LORIE LINE

and her Pop Chamber O

Selections from

SHARING *the* SEASON

VOLUME III

Piano Arrangements and Orchestrations by Lorie Line

Edited by Anita Ruth

©1995 Lorie Line Music, Inc.
222 Minnetonka Avenue South   Wayzata, MN 55391   (952) 474-1000
www.lorieline.com

NOTES FROM THE ARTIST

Thinking back and reflecting on the holidays, what I remember most as a child is eating oven roasted turkey and homemade peanut brittle, giving and receiving gifts, laughing and digging out the Christmas carols … me, of course playing them on the piano for my family, and all of us trying to sing four-part harmony. We usually ended up giggling so hard that someone had to make a quick dart to the bathroom, or crying because the music really was beautiful. I loved the holiday season as a child, because it was the one special time of year when everyone would gather around the piano and I wouldn't be by myself, just practicing. I never imagined that as an adult, I'd be sharing holiday music with the world, making spirits bright.

Sharing the Season, Volume III is intended to do just that. In each song I have tried to bring to you a different musical influence, and I hope you will enjoy the variety of sounds. There's something here for everyone.

May this music put tears in your eyes and a smile on your face. May it help you recall sentimental memories and happy times too. May it provide you with times of reflection and moments of celebration. And may it set the mood for creating many meaningful and lasting memories for you to enjoy, each holiday season to come.

Merry Christmas to all!

Lorie Line

Lorie Line

ABOUT THE COVER

The angel on the front cover was painted by Robert A. Olson, a leader in the genre "romantic realism." He is nationally known for his fine art limited edition music prints. His European study of the Old Masters has had a marked influence on his style and methods of painting. Mr. Olson has amassed some 30 awards for his artwork.

TABLE OF CONTENTS

❦

Carol of the Bells

Hark! how the bells; Sweet silver bells,
　All seem to say "Throw cares away"
Christmas is here Bringing good cheer
　To young and old, Meek and the bold
Ding, dong, ding, dong, That is their song,
　With joyful ring, All caroling.
One seems to hear, Words of good cheer,
　From everywhere, Filling the air
O, how they pound, Raising the sound,
　O'er hill and dale, Telling their tale,
Gayly they ring, While people sing
　song of good cheer, Christmas is here!
Merry, merry, merry, Merry Christmas!
　Merry, merry, merry, Merry Christmas!
On, on they send, on without end
　their joyful tone to every home.
Ding, dong, ding, dong.

As With Gladness

As with gladness men of old
　Did the guiding star behold;
As with joy they hailed its light,
　Leading onward, beaming bright;
So, most gracious Lord, may we
　Evermore be led to Thee.

As with joyful steps they sped
　To that lowly manger bed,
There to bend the knee before
　Him whom heaven and earth adore;
So may we with willing feet
　Ever seek Thy mercy seat.

As they offered gifts most rare,
　At that manger rude and bare,
So may we with holy joy,
　Pure and free from sin's alloy,
All our costliest treasures bring,
　Christ, to Thee, our heavenly King.

Go Tell It On the Mountain

When I was a seeker,
　I sought both night and day,
I sought the Lord to help me,
　and He showed me the way,
Oh! Go tell it on the mountain,
　over the hills and ev'rywhere,
Go tell it on the mountain
　that Jesus Christ is born!
He made me a watchman
　upon the city wall,
And if I am a Christian,
　I am the least of all,
Oh! Go tell it on the mountain,
　over the hills and ev'rywhere,
Go tell it on the mountain,
　that Jesus Christ is born!

Once In Royal David's City

Once in royal David's city
　Stood a lowly cattle shed,
Where a mother laid her Baby
　In a manger for His bed:
Mary was that mother mild,
　Jesus Christ her little Child.

He came down to earth from heaven,
　Who is God and Lord of all,
And His shelter was a stable,
　And His cradle was a stall:
With the poor, and mean, and lowly,
　Lived on earth our Savior holy.

Jesus is our childhood's pattern,
　Day by day like us He grew;
He was little, weak, and helpless,
　Tears and smiles, like us, He knew:
And He feeleth for our sadness,
　And He shareth in our gladness.

And our eyes at last shall see Him,
　Through His own redeeming love,
For that Child so dear and gentle
　Is our Lord in heav'n above:
And He leads His children on
　To the place where He is gone.

Gesu Bambino

When blossoms flowered 'mid the snows
　upon a winter night,
Was born the Child the Christmas rose
　the King of love and light.
The angels sang, the shepherds sang,
　the grateful earth rejoiced,
And at His blessed birth,
　the stars their exultation voiced.

Oh come let us adore him,
　Oh come let us adore him,
Oh come let us adore him,
　Christ the Lord.

Again the heart with rapture glows
　to greet the Holy night,
That gave the world its Christmas rose,
　its King of love and light.
Let every voice acclaim His name,
　the grateful chorus swell
From Paradise to Earth He came,
　that we with Him might dwell.

Carol of the Bells

Arranged by LORIE LINE
and PETER OSTROUSHKO
Edited by Anita Ruth

With bright, whirling motion

6

Harmonica Solo

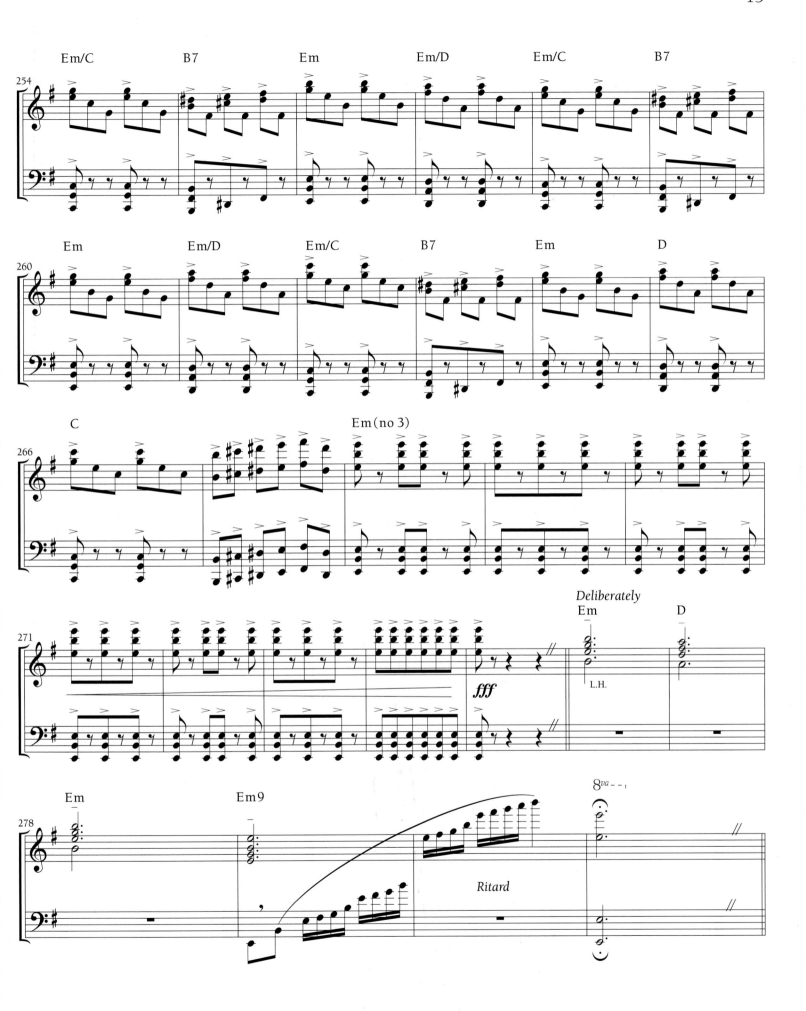

14

As With Gladness

Arranged by LORIE LINE
Edited by Anita Ruth

Quietly

Guitar Lead (Optional)

GUITAR

As With Gladness

Arranged by *LORIE LINE*
Edited by Anita Ruth

Go Tell It On the Mountain

Arranged by LORIE LINE

Edited by Anita Ruth

Slowly, in a reflective manner

Harmonica Solo   (Optional)

Tenor Sax Solo   *(Optional)*

Once In Royal David's City

Arranged by LORIE LINE

Edited by Anita Ruth

Dancing with anticipation

Flowing, moving ahead

Mandolin Solo (Optional)

Guitar Solo (Optional)

WINDS

Once In Royal David's City

Arranged by LORIE LINE

Edited by Anita Ruth

Dancing with anticipation

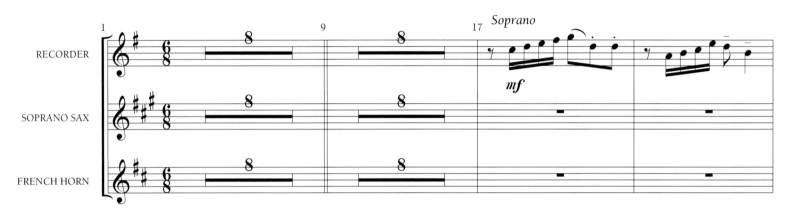

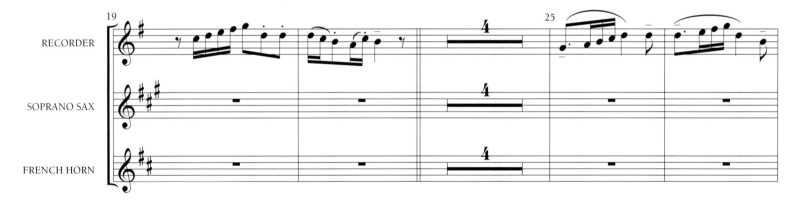

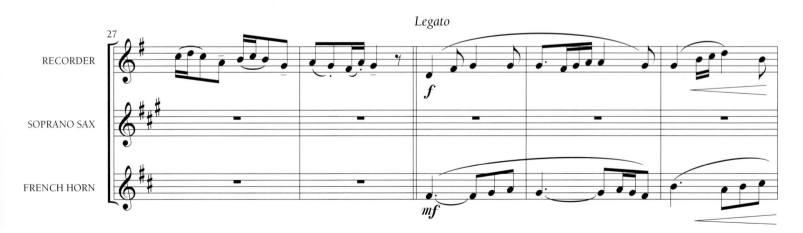

Once In Royal David's City

Arranged by LORIE LINE
Edited by Anita Ruth

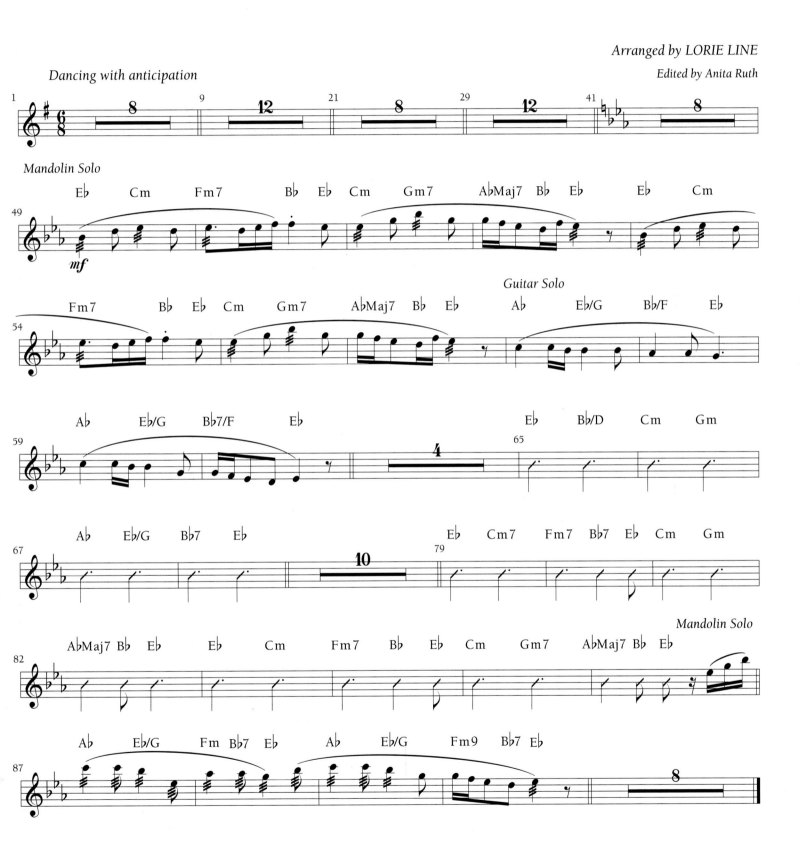

Once In Royal David's City

Arranged by LORIE LINE

Edited by Anita Ruth

Dancing with anticipation

Gesu Bambino

Arranged by LORIE LINE
Edited by Anita Ruth

Sweetly, with childlike innocence

Mandolin Solo   (Optional)

WINDS

Gesu Bambino

Sweetly, with childlike innocence

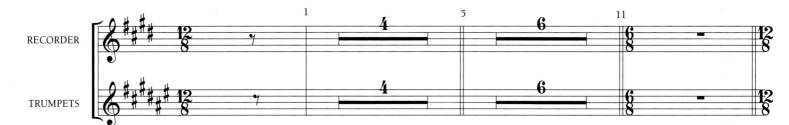

RHYTHM

Gesu Bambino

Arranged by LORIE LINE

Edited by Anita Ruth

Sweetly, with childlike innocence

Mandolin Solo

STRINGS

Gesu Bambino

Arranged by LORIE LINE

Edited by Anita Ruth

Sweetly, with childlike innocence

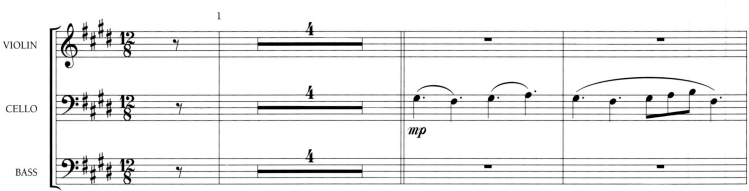

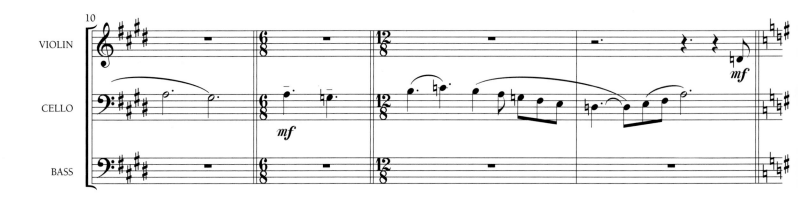

50

The *Lorie Line* Music Collection

Young At Heart
The Classics, Volume I
Solo and Orchestrated Piano

The first volume in a series, this brand new release *Young At Heart* features great standards in a piano trio format. Performed with a small ensemble, each song reflects Lorie's personal piano style. The album includes great timeless favorites like *Misty, Autumn Leaves, Summertime, The Nearness of You, Smile, As Time Goes By, Young At Heart* (the title track), and many more.

Available in CD and Music Book.

Open House
Orchestrated Piano

Over one hour of intimate piano music, performed solo and with simple accompaniment featuring originals, Celtic and Irish music, traditionals and popular show tunes.

Available in CD and Music Book.

Best Seller!
Music from the Heart
Solo and Orchestrated Piano

Features 17 of the most requested contemporary standards from movies and Broadway in Lorie's recognizable style. This is a compilation of the best and most well-known songs.

Available in CD and Music Book.

Best Seller!
Threads of Love
Solo and Orchestrated Piano

Definitely Lorie's best selling album.

Available in CD and Sheet Music Singles.

Threads of Love
Rondo
From the Heart

Beyond A Dream
Solo and Orchestrated Piano

Some of the best cover tunes plus two original pieces from Lorie.

Available in CD and Sheet Music Single.

Beyond A Dream

Just Me
Solo Piano

This album combines the top two favorite areas of Lorie's music together—solo piano and all-original. *Just Me* features Lorie's own compositions without accompaniment in her very personal and heartwarming style. Features 14 original songs which are sure to be favorites.

Available in CD and Music Book.

Walking With You
Solo and Orchestrated Piano

A mixture of classic, popular and original tunes.

Available in CD and Music Book.

Heart and Soul
Orchestrated Piano

This is fully orchestrated and features visual melody lines that are memorable and heartwarming. This all-original album is a 1995 release, has been on the charts in "Billboard" magazine and it features members of Lorie's Pop Chamber Orchestra.

Available in CD and Music Book.

Simply Grand
Solo Piano

This one hour recording features some of the most romantic music of all time plus Lorie Line originals. *Simply Grand* reflects its title in the purest form—simple and grand. Fifteen songs.

Available in CD and Music Book.

Lorie Line Live! Best Seller!
Solo Piano Music Book

Eighty pages of solo piano music from Lorie's first national PBS television special. Features the most requested and popular music from Lorie and highlights from her popular original album, *Heart and Soul*. A Best Seller!

Available in Music Book only.

The Heritage Collection
Volume III
Orchestrated Piano

Features some of the most beloved historic American music, patriotic songs and classic and timeless hymns. A fully orchestrated album, this music is very "fresh", emotionally moving and sometimes very exciting. Over one hour of music, 16 songs!

Available in CD and Music Book.

The Heritage Collection
Volume I
Solo and Orchestrated Piano

Uplifting songs and hymns from our heritage.

Available in CD and Music Book.

The Show Stoppers
Orchestrated Piano with Vocal Performance

Robert Robinson performs with Lorie Line & her Pop Chamber Orchestra. For 10 years Lorie Line has toured with her Pop Chamber Orchestra. In the makeup of this group has been a very special person, vocalist Robert Robinson. When he joined the tour in 1992, the show would never be the same. He had the gift to bring people to tears and to their feet, night after night. His voice literally stopped the show with applause every night in every city.

Available in CD only.

The Heritage Collection
Volume II
Solo and Orchestrated Piano

Sixteen timeless piano arrangements, featuring songs of inspiration. One hour of music.

Available in CD and Music Book.

The Big Band
Sharing The Season
Volume Four
Orchestrated Piano

This recording is the most fully orchestrated big band album ever recorded by Lorie & her Pop Chamber Orchestra. In high contrast to an intimate solo piano recording, this album is "big", high energy, and lots of fun! It reflects the personality of a live show. You will find your toes tapping and your fingers snapping when you listen to this music. Features over one hour of music, 16 songs!

Available in CD and Music Book.

Sharing The Season
Volume I
Solo and Orchestrated Piano

Features 15 classic and traditional holiday songs: *Silent Night, It Came Upon A Midnight Clear, Oh Come Little Children, Away In A Manger* and many more Christmas favorites.

Available in CD and Music Book.

Sharing The Season
Volume III
Orchestrated Piano

This holiday album features Lorie's upbeat material performed on her holiday tour. It is a joyous recording, showcasing unique styles and cultural influences. This is one of Lorie's personal favorite holiday albums and a best seller.

Available in CD and Music Book.

The Silver Album
Solo Piano Holiday Favorites

This is the first solo piano holiday album ever to be released by Lorie. The entire album is easy-listening and features 16 classics and favorites: *White Christmas, O Tannenbaum, Angels From The Realms Of Glory, Bells Over Bethlehem, The Christmas Song, Have A Holly Jolly Christmas* and more.

Available in CD and Music Book.

Sharing The Season
Volume II
Solo and Orchestrated Piano

If you're tired of the same ol' Christmas songs, this orchestrated piano album features traditional holiday songs, some of which may be new to you.

Available in CD and Music Book.

Best Seller!
Home For The Holidays
Solo Piano Music Book

Fifteen solo piano arrangements of Lorie's most popular holiday songs from her *Sharing The Season* albums. A Best Seller!

Available in Music Book only.